Stars of One Heaven

Melanie Lotfali

Clara was all alone.
Clara was lonely.
She looked up at the sky.
She saw the sky was full of stars.

She turned to one and said:
"You are so lucky.
You have so many friends.
I am all alone.
I want a friend."

Star said: "Clara, why don't you ask God for a friend?"

So Clara prayed. She asked God to send her a friend.

When she opened her eyes she saw that God had sent her a friend.

"Oh no!" said Clara.
"I want a friend just like me! He is different from me!"

Clara closed her eyes and prayed again.

Then, she opened her eyes.

"Oh no!" sobbed Clara.

"I want a friend just like me! She is different from me!"

Clara closed her eyes and prayed again.

Then, she opened her eyes.

"Oh no!" cried Clara.

"I want a friend just LIKE ME!

She is DIFFERENT from me!"

Clara threw herself on the grass.

She cried and cried.

The new friends wandered away.

That night she turned to Star.
"Why does God keep sending me the wrong thing?" she asked.

Star said to Clara:
"When you look up to the sky, what do you see?"

Clara said: "I see beautiful stars shining brightly."

Star said: "That's right. We are all different shapes, colors, and sizes. But when you look up you see our unity. You see we are all stars."

"When I look down," said Star,
"I see beautiful human beings.
It doesn't matter that you
are different shapes, colors, and sizes.
You are all human beings."

"Oh yes!" laughed Clara.
"Now, where did they go,
those friends just like me?"

...love will make them all the stars of one heaven.

~ Bahá'í Writings ~

Copyright © 2013 Melanie Lotfali

Stars of One Heaven
by Melanie Lotfali is licensed
under a Creative Commons
Attribution-NonCommercial-ShareAlike 4.0
International License.

ISBN 978-0-9945925-0-6

www.ingramcontent.com/pod-product-compliance
Lightning Source LLC
Chambersburg PA
CBHW061938290426
44113CB00025B/2948